THE RECKLESS WIND

Where and when to find nice and gorgeous women

Daniel A. Nathaniel

Table of content

Chapter 1

Where to Meet Women and Create an Abundant Dating Life

I'm going to teach you, step-by-step, how and where to meet more women in the next 90 days than you've met all your life. And to top it off, create a lifestyle that naturally attracts the women you are most attracted to.

Instead of giving you a trite list of the best places to meet women (that you've read dozens of times before), I'm going to teach you what no other article will...

Exactly how to set up your lifestyle and social network to effortlessly attract high-quality women to you.

Not only will you learn where to meet women, but I'll teach you the exact mindsets and strategies I've personally used to become "That Guy", elevate your social status, and become a leader women are uncontrollably drawn to.

By the time you're done, you'll have a proven strategy for creating an amazing life filled with close friends, powerful allies, and, of course, stunning women.

Let's dive in.

What Billionaire Real Estate Investors Can Teach You About Meeting Women where to meet single women image
There's an old saying in the real estate community that success comes down to three things...

Location. Location. Location!

As cliche as it might be, it's true. And the same principle applies when trying to create a successful dating life.

You can be the epitome of a Grounded Man...

you can have a jawline like an Abercrombie model, a body like Thor, a booming bank account, a contagious smile, and enough charisma to make Dwayne Johnson look like Steve Erkel...

...

But if you live in an area where few or no high-quality women live, these "assets" will never be seen. So to the women you most desire, it's not a matter of "more" resources, you simply don't exist.

Therefore, the first question to ask yourself when trying to find the best places to meet women is: "Do I live in a city where women are abundant...especially high-quality women?"

You don't need to live in Los Angeles or NYC (although it doesn't hurt), but you must live in a city that attracts the kinds of women you are attracted to.

If your goal is to date a stunning model or a beautiful boss babe, you'll be hard-pressed to find her living in a rural town in Northern Kansas.

Now, you might be thinking to yourself, "I get what you're saying...but you don't expect me to uproot my life and move to a whole new city just to meet higher-quality women, do you?"

Yes, I do.

But not only for women. It's crucial to evaluate the "hidden" advantages of living in a larger city or an up-and-coming metropolis... even if such advantages come with (what appears to be) a price.

For example, if you were to relocate to San Diego (where I reside) from a tiny town in the South, you would likely be compelled to decrease your living environment. My rent here in Pacific Beach for a two-bedroom apartment is more than many 5-bedroom houses with a pool in the Midwest.

But...

The enjoyable lifestyle, caliber of people, and enhanced quality of life make the trade-off worth it by a factor of 10.

Instead of living in an oversized home (of which I would use less than 25 percent) as a status symbol to boost my ego, I decided to live in a modest apartment that's only three blocks from the beach, ten minutes from downtown (and some of the best nightlife in the country), and surrounded by more adventurous activities than I can count.

Whether I want to hike around ocean cliffs, surf with the sunrise, sail the San Diego Bay, or enjoy some of the best Mexican food in the country...

I can. Because I've built my life to surround myself with excellent people and enjoyable activities over vacant beds and unneeded square footage.

Another additional advantage of living in a larger city is that it's simpler to network with better quality men, develop a flourishing social circle, and enhance your profession.

Because I opted to reside in San Diego, I've been able to establish an extraordinary network filled with multi-millionaires, actual high-performers of their industry, and stunning ladies.

While it's true that living in a major city like LA or NYC will require you to compete against higher-caliber guys, relocating some place like Austin, TX, or Scottsdale, AZ enables you to enjoy the best of both worlds. You'll have a surplus of great ladies and you won't be battling for their attention against movie producers, celebrities, and big shot entrepreneurs.

Sometimes, a single action is all it takes to shift the direction of your whole life (including, of course, your romantic future) (and of course, your romantic future). And if you're willing to relocate to a larger city and go out simply a few times a week, I guarantee, your dating life will drastically improve because of it.

How to Find the Best Place to Meet Women: Look for the "Golden Ratio"

As a quick side note, if you're considering moving close to a nearby city or jetting halfway across the country to find a home base that supports the lifestyle you desire and allows you to meet more women...

...You must learn the ratio of the city where you plan to go to make sure you're living in the greatest spot to meet ladies.

If you live in a city with more men than women–even if the city has thousands of beautiful women–you're setting yourself up for a challenge.

When the population of a city is weighted toward men, the women in that city will have their "pick of the litter", which tends to breed entitlement among women and machismo-fueled competition among men. These ladies are "picked up" all the time which means you will need outstanding social skills and knowledge of attraction to succeed.

Being average will provide even below average outcomes if in a city with ratios of more males than women.

This is not to argue it's impossible to succeed with high-quality women in these cities…

simply that you need to be on your A-game and expect that there will be competition.

If you want to develop your social abilities, understand the "lost secrets" of attraction, and establish a rich dating life filled with wonderful ladies.

So bear this in mind before jumping ship and going to a new city. Go visit the city first and talk to the locals to get a better idea of the community and where it's headed.

When most guys say, "I don't know where to meet women!" what they are saying 90 percent of the time is, "I'm not willing to put myself in a position to meet the women I really desire...is there anywhere I can go where women will approach me and do all of the hard work?"

The simple truth, assuming you live in a metropolitan area or a well-populated city that is growing, attractive women are everywhere! You see them at the coffee shop, walking their dogs at local parks, and working out five feet away from you at the gym. But it's up to you to take the first move and begin the contact.

Let me repeat. It's not the woman's business to approach males. It's yours!

During the day, you may meet women:

Doing something healthy and active: Gyms, yoga, jogging, fitness classes, healthy eating restaurants.

Doing something entertaining and social:
Day drinking, parties, live music, festivals,
lounging out by the pool/beach
Doing something adventurous: trekking,
standup paddle boarding, surfing
Running errands: grocery shops, shopping
malls.
At night, you may discover high-quality
ladies at:

Trendy restaurants
Bars, lounges, theaters, and clubs
House parties
And of course, you can discover a wealth of
stunning, high-quality women, day or night
on social media and dating applications like
Tinder, Bumble, Match, and Hinge.

But there's a problem…

You already know where to meet women.
You knew about all of these places before
you even clicked on this article. And I'd
guess that you probably don't want to go out

to bars or clubs every night to meet new women (women who are likely in a stage where you don't want to be in a long-term relationship)... you want something more unique, authentic, something more original.

The real challenge you're facing is not figuring out where to meet women...but rather how to meet women naturally and authentically instead of relying on canned lines, forced conversations, or gimmicky routines.

This is why I encourage you to take a new approach to meet women. An approach that allows you to naturally attract women into your life instead of feeling the need to go out and "pull" them in.

An approach that will not only help you meet more women...but will improve your social life and help you become more attractive...automatically.

A New Approach to Meeting Women (and the Hidden Dangers of the "Man Cave") best places to meet women's image
To effortlessly meet and attract new high-quality women into your life, you need to challenge the old approach of simply going to the bar or sitting around the coffee shop waiting for a cute girl to walk in and take notice of you permitting you to meet her.

You need to create a new approach that meshes effortlessly with your lifestyle and allows you to meet the women you want without going out of your way to do it.

Luckily, this "new approach" is effortlessly simple (and a helluva lot of fun!)

The "secret" to making this new approach work for you is to shift your lifestyle from a passive consumer of entertainment (what 95 percent of men do in their free time) to be actively engaged with the city you live in and spending more time doing interesting and adventurous things.

Treat your entire city like your backyard and a part of your home vs this rare place you seldom explore except for when friends or family are in town.

Many men who struggle to meet the women they want aren't "bad" at meeting or interacting with women. They've simply fallen into a blaze lifestyle centered around "success" and or mindless entertainment instead of adventure, exploration, and connection.

They wake up, drive to work, hustle hard, come home exhausted, and then look forward to grabbing a beer, turning on the TV, or playing Xbox to keep themselves occupied until they're ready to fall asleep. They aren't doing anything in their day-to-day lives that breathe aliveness into their everyday life and, as a result, they have a lackluster (or nonexistent) social life and very few opportunities to meet the women they want to date.

Ironically, the more a man finds success in his career, and grows his income the more he expands his lifestyle to make "going out" all but obsolete.

Let me explain...

Instead of going out during the day or night to entertain himself, he relaxes in his custom-built "man cave", playing video games or watching movies on his mounted 72" television with surround sound speakers in every crevice of the home...

Instead of going out to a coffee shop and enjoying a lazy Saturday morning meeting new people or catching up with a friend, he buys a $1,000 Espresso machine so he can enjoy the best "Cup of Joe" from the comfort of his own home...

Instead of going to a popular gym or taking group workout classes, he builds an expensive garage gym so he can make those "gains" without ever leaving his home or apartment...

Instead of going out to bars or a lounge, he builds a lavish in-home bar (complete with all his favorite whiskeys and wines), billiards, and pool table and spends his Saturday nights drinking solo or with one or maybe two friends.

Most men aren't consciously aware that their "man cave" is limiting their lifestyle and, counterintuitively, reducing their desire to go out and meet new women. But the fact remains...the more incentive you have to stay in, the fewer women you will meet and the lonelier your life will be.

The longer this "man cave" lifestyle persists the harder it becomes for him to get out of the cave and back into the real world to engage with life.

Eventually, men will associate enjoying life with spending time in the "man cave", and going out becomes this weird activity that is rarely done and reserved for special occasions only.

The solution is simple...

Find your entertainment outside of your home. Instead of turning to devices and luxuries that cradle (read: trap) you in your tiny bubble... commit to going out, exploring, connecting, and sharing with others on a more frequent basis.

Treat your home or apartment the same way you would treat a hotel room on vacation. It's simply there for you to sleep, eat, and get ready for the future day's trip. The hotel is not meant for you to spend all your free time, watching movies in bed and ordering room service.

To help you get the most out of this, here are a few tactical ways you can apply this "social life first" lifestyle.

The Foundational Pillars of Meeting Women Organically\swhere to meet women's image To begin building a lifestyle that makes it easy to meet women (and have a ton of fun), we're going to start with a few foundational lifestyle "pillars".

By taking action on the following strategies, you'll be able to meet more women without spending a fortune on cover charges, users, and bottle service...

and you'll be able to meet higher quality women as a natural byproduct of your lifestyle.

1. Barbells vs. Bars: A Simple Tactic to Meet Higher Quality Women While Improving Your Life

First, I encourage you to sign up for multiple gyms and fitness centers in your area. I know this might sound expensive, but when you do the math...it isn't. And, because of the efficacy of this method, I'm going to spend a little bit more time discussing it.

Think of it like this...

If the average gym in your area charges $40/month for membership–the industry average–and you sign up for three different gyms that offer a variety of different classes, activities, and "vibes" (e.g. CrossFit, yoga classes, group workouts, etc), you're paying $120/month to have access to healthy environments that make it easy to meet quality women.

And...you may go to any of these gyms many days out of the week and join courses where

you can meet stunning single ladies every
single day.

Now, compare this to the normal fare of
going to a bar or club simply twice a week.

Not only will you have fewer possibilities to
meet high-quality women—because you're
only going out twice a week and the women
you tend to meet in these areas are typically
not in the correct frame of mind for a
relationship—but you'll be spending twice as
much to do it.

If you have just three drinks a night and
they cost $8 on average...you're looking at
more than $190/month just to go out twice
a week and compete against dozens of other
men for the attention of a few party girls.

That doesn't even take Uber rides, cover
charges, "buying rounds", tipping, and
late-night food into account. When you add
all of these expenses up, you'll likely be

spending more than $400/month or more for a few nights of inebriated "fun" often meeting zero women in the whole process!

Also, it's important to consider the quality of the interactions you can have at a gym/fitness center vs. a bar or club. It's easier to strike up a conversation with a woman with whom you shared an experience after a challenging hot yoga session or intense CrossFit workout than it is to cold approach a group of girls at the bar (who've already been approached by five other dudes and are on defense).

In my experience, the most intelligent, attractive, and grounded women all take care of their bodies. I have yet to meet a truly stunning and interesting woman who does not exercise regularly.

And, of course, those extra memberships will come with the added benefit of keeping you in shape and ensuring that you're taking steps to become a healthier and more grounded man.

2. Why Paleo Buffs and Ketogenic Dieters Have an Easier Time Meeting Women
Some of the best places to meet women during the day (with almost no competition from other men) are trendy healthy grocery stores like Trader Joe's, Whole Foods, Earth Fare, Sprouts, and your local farmer's market.

Although I rarely do my full grocery shopping at these stores (I get 80 percent of my food delivered with Amazon prime now), every time I go out to buy a new bag of coffee or local avocado or raw honey...

I see at least one woman who catches my attention.

Throughout the week, make a point to grab at least a few specialty items from a local "healthy food" store (even if you do the brunt of your shopping elsewhere) and you'll be surprised at the quality of women you can meet frequenting these places.

3. Hack Your "Administrative Time" to Meet New Women and Be More Productive
Another easy way to start meeting women during the day is to go to trendy coffee shops, juice stores, bookstores, or happy hour bars to check your email, read, and relax for an hour or so.

Instead of sitting in your office or on your couch, isolated and cut off from the rest of the world, save any "low brainpower" activities (like checking email, handling administrative work, reading, or even journaling) in a trendy public spot where you can find women to meet.

Not only will you likely be more productive (according to studies) but you'll have an easier time meeting the types of women

you're interested in since it's naturally a part
of your day, not forced.

4. Tap into the Hidden Power of "Referrals"
to Meet New Women Automatically
One of my "underground" secrets for
effortlessly meeting amazing women is to
leverage my social circle to ask for
"referrals".

If you have a social circle of friends, it's
relatively easy to find single women in your
network who are interested in meeting you.

By simply asking a close friend or his
girlfriend if they have any single friends who
might be a good fit in your life, you can set
up a few dates and meet women by simply
asking. Of course, you need to consider how
you can return the value to your friend.

As a bonus, getting a referral from a friend
instantly elevates your social status and
makes the first date a lot easier.

Seriously…

Pull out your phone right now and shoot off a message to 2-3 friends.

"Hey I was wondering if you knew any single women that might be interested in doing X activity with us this weekend, friends of friends, co-workers, etc, feel free to invite?"

You'll be amazed by what happens next.

5. Swipe Your Way to a Better Social Life Finally, we have online dating. Although I don't encourage you to rely on apps like Tinder, Hinge, or Bumble to meet women (especially because of the competition from other men and types of women these platforms tend to attract), you would be a fool not to use technology to your advantage.

You simply can't be everywhere in your city at once, but online dating apps allow you to expand your reach and meet women you otherwise would not have meant.

By spending just 10-minutes a day swiping and messaging (likely while you're on "The White Throne"), you can meet and set up a date with a few women a month.

Advanced Strategies for Meeting Women and Becoming "The Source" to Effortlessly Attract High-Quality Women meeting women the easy way image
By implementing just a few of the "foundational lifestyle pillars", you'll be well on your way to meeting more women and setting up more dates.

But what if there was a "shortcut"? An advanced strategy that allowed you to not only meet high-quality women in your daily life but to actively pull high-quality women into your life in a way that gave you an "unfair" advantage and immediately put you at the top of the social food chain?

Well...there is. I call this strategy "Being the Source" and it works like this...

First, I want you to think of an activity that you enjoy. Something that you would do by yourself but that women also tend to enjoy.

Once you have a few ideas, ask yourself, "How can I host one of these activities on my own and lead an event that will naturally draw in amazing women?"

For example, one of my good friends (who's a massive yoga nut) decided to start hosting a free sunset yoga class every week in Pacific Beach.

When he first started this event, he would have fewer than three attendees...

and all of them were other men. But he kept at it, "marketed" the event by posting on social media, taking great photos, and encouraging his friends to bring their friends today...he has more than 100 students show up every week... and almost 70% of them are women that live within 5 miles of the event location, which happens to be nearby his house.

Because he's in a position of leadership (he's the organizer and host of the event), women are naturally drawn to him and he'll regularly have at least 5 women approach him after the class is over practically begging him if he wants to meet up for drinks or hang out later.

He's going on more dates than ever before, never has to "force" himself to go to the bar when he doesn't want to, and genuinely enjoys hosting the event every week, with or without women.

where to meet women during the day image
A photo from my friend's yoga class
Therefore, the best place to meet women is
by creating a social group that women
naturally want to be a part of where they are
in a position of leadership.

Organizing and leading events like these
aren't easy. And most men aren't willing to
be patient and put in the hard work required
to run them even when it seems no progress
is being made.

So if you're willing to stick with it and create
something like this, you'll stand head and
shoulders above other men and create a fun
weekly gathering that allows you to
effortlessly attract the women you're most
interested in.

Jot down a few ideas for events to meet
women that you could host right now. A few
ideas:

Weekly running group
Weekly yoga group
Weekly "Bootcamp" exercise
Weekly bar crawl
Weekly improv group\sWeekly hiking group
Weekly cooking lessons
Weekly surfing lessons
Weekly book club (cheesy, but it works)
(cheesy, but it works).
Take action now to get this event happening.
Text five friends and ask them to come out
(and bring a +1), post on social media, and
then get started. It could take you a few
months or longer, but if you stick with it,
your weekly group/event might provide you
access to dozens of great women each
month–all of whom will be attracted to you
because of your position as a leader.

To take this to the next level, I encourage
you to start befriending men of influence in
your area and building your social circles
around them. Instead of trying to figure out
where to meet women by yourself and

competing with men of status and prestige, turn these men into your allies and work together as a team to build incredible social circles full of attractive women.

When you can meet and befriend high-status men who simply don't have the time to meet women but have the resources to create fun experiences. You can become a duo where you organize and bring together women and the higher-status men often gladly pay for the experiences.

Women want to be a part of elite groups and come alongside men who are doing adventurous and fun things with their lives. By expanding your social circle, you can become one of the leaders of those groups and set yourself apart from the masses of men using cheesy pickup lines and canned routines on the streets late at night.

You'll also be privy to private events and gatherings like clothing label launches, restaurant openings, fashion weeks, and luxurious house parties. At events like these, it's much easier to meet women because the exclusivity of the event signifies that you must be "in the know" and a part of the "Who's who" in your area.

This is an especially effective way to meet women as you get older where going to bars/clubs late at night becomes unappealing.

You can meet high-quality women by reaching out to a "uber-successful" friend or colleague who has an amazing high-rise penthouse, beachfront mansion, or just a great place to throw events and offer to organize and host a party at his house.

What most men don't appreciate is that males in the top 1 percent want to have fun and be the center of attention as much as everyone else...

however, they frequently lack the time and energy to put up such activities.

By volunteering to arrange everything and lead the event, you will have the chance to meet more great ladies and he will get to throw enjoyable parties without spending your financial resources. It's a win-win for both of you and will likely develop your connection further since you are delivering a mutually beneficial benefit to each other.

Finally, I advise you to tap into the power of "Sociable Lites"…highly social and high-status persons of influence in your neighborhood including party promoters, yoga teachers (at really fashionable studios), restaurant/bar owners, and DJs.

It takes effort to create relationships with these sorts of individuals and you'll need to be creative to uncover methods you can bring value to them (remember…the more value you give, the more you receive). But when you have an "inner circle" populated with the finest grade guys nearby, you will obtain unlimited access to the greatest-quality women in your community.

When you befriend these sorts of famous guys, you can create and participate in wonderful activities that women naturally want to be a part of.

Remember the Golden Rule of Meeting Women (Or Doom Yourself to Failure) (Or Doom Yourself to Failure)
By employing the methods and ideas I've outlined above, you can and will start meeting more women than you ever imagined possible.

But I want to make things clear...

You do NOT have to apply all I've given in this post.

Unless you aim to become the "Dan Bilzerian" of your region and constantly party with bikini models...you just need to identify 1-2 tactics that work for you and follow them consistently. Most of you reading this are only looking for one great woman with whom you can share your life.

You don't need 100 or 20 or even 5 ladies. Just one (maybe two lol) (maybe two hehe).

So take a deep breath, relax and remove the strain you're experiencing right now.

You don't need to use every strategy and you don't need to use any of them indefinitely.

My goal in writing this article was to reframe the way you think about meeting women and where you can find women to help you realize that you don't need to hit a bar or club every night to have a fun social circle filled with high-quality people. You may perform all of the above sober if you choose.

Whatever you decide to do, remember...this is intended to be enjoyable!

If you aren't having fun, you're doing it wrong and you will all but guarantee you never meet the women you're most interested in.

So take everything I've taught you today about meeting women and use it in a manner that makes sense for your dating objectives. Create a lifestyle that you like and that enables you to meet the ladies you desire organically.

Truthfully, you're only one lifestyle shift away from meeting the woman of your dreams.

Now go take action, enjoy yourself, and start meeting the women you've always desired.

Chapter 2

FOUR ASPECTS OF VALUES ARE AS FOLLOWS:

1. General and Specific Values:

(a) General Values:

Values such as democracy, freedom, the right to dissent, respect for fundamental rights and dignity of work, etc., for example, are quite universal.

These ideals are abstract and they permeate many facets of life. A high number of values are discovered to be quite universal. Sociologically, they are more important.

(b) Specific Values:

Values are typically articulated in precise language. For example, we may value physical health or prosperity. More precisely, we may favor silk above nylon or the work of a certain author over that of another. Values generally vary from extremely abstract to specific levels.

2. Values are hierarchical arranged:\sAll the values are not equally important. We may create a difference between-'Means Values', 'Ends Values', 'Dominant Values', and 'Ultimate Values,

(a) 'Means Values' are instrumental values. They are desired as part of the endeavor to accomplish other ideals,

(b) 'Ends Values' are broader and more significant from the point of view of the organizations that are undertaking the valuing task.

For example, if health is the value, then the maintenance of a healthy diet, obtaining sufficient rest, avoidance of alcoholic beverages and drug addictions, completing correct workouts consistently, etc., become means to that aim. This distinction is depending on circumstances and situations. But it enables us to grasp how the values are patterned and how one is connected to another.

(c) 'Dominant Values' are those values that impact and shape the conduct of individuals to a large degree. Sociologist Williams has offered the following criteria for prevailing values:

I Extensiveness. Whether the value is substantially discovered in the overall activities of the people?
(ii) Duration. Whether the value has been lasting and seen over a lengthy period?
(iii) Intensity. With what intensity the value is sought or maintained by the people?
(iv) Prestige of Value Carriers: To what degree do the value bearers such as individuals, goods, or organizations have a reputation in society? For example, 'sacrifice' and 'service' are two of many major values in Indian society. Similarly, 'individual enterprise' and 'success in life' are two dominating ideals of American culture.

(d) The 'Ultimate Values' relate to those values of the organization that offers purpose, substance, and direction to the lives of individuals.

Example:\sIf we take the above-mentioned example of physical health we may argue, that it is essential for lifespan. Longevity or extended life span may be justified in terms of 'ultimate value' to offer service to mankind and to be worthy of God's creation. There can be no greater or more ultimate worth than this.

3. Explicit and Implicit Values:\sMost of the societal values are declared and openly embraced. They are actively taught to the youngsters. Through official, governmental, and other organizational ways they are reinforced to the grownups. They are also promoted via the media. Examples: democracy, freedom, fundamental rights, social equality, etc. These principles are expressly held and valued.

Some of the ideals are implicitly embraced by the people. Public officials, spokespeople for the society, and even religious leaders may not focus on this greatly. They may even disregard them. For example, respect for elders and conformity, taking care of aged parents, and respect for authority are values implicitly accepted in our culture.

4. Values may Conflict with One Another:\sValues may frequently conflict with one another. In complex civilizations, we often witness not just one value system but more than one. We discover various, overlapping and sometimes even antagonistic value systems in the same culture. For example, the right to dissent, conformity, respect for authority, and respect for elders-are principles that are in conflict.

Some of the values are possibly contradicting. When they are prevalent, it becomes hard for us to pursue some of them without violating others. For example, we value religious worship for personal fulfillment. At the same time, we equally value attainment of status, acquisition of riches, etc. Here, the first one may collide with the latter.

Normally, in a contemporary complex society, we encounter conflict between groups who espouse mutually opposing beliefs. For example, some may value patriotism, respect for authority, and disapprove of dissent.

Some people may attach considerable weight to the value of establishing peace. For them, establishing peace is more vital than surrendering to or accepting the war plans of their country leaders.

No surprise, if, at times, the first group conflicts with the second. In the same manner, during the British rule in India, while some Indian nationals preferred to cherish the values of "respect for authority" and "obedience to the master "; some others dedicated themselves to upholding the values of 'independence' and fundamental liberties'.

It seems reasonable to assume that there are fewer value conflicts in small homogeneous societies than in large heterogeneous ones.